THE ILLINOIS CENTRAL RAILROAD

by Robert K. Durham

2000
Published by Robert K. Durham
Printed in the USA

OTHER BOOKS BY THE AUTHOR

New York Central Steam
Erie Steam
Pennsylvania Steam
Baltimore & Ohio Steam
Jersey Central Steam
Seaboard Air Line Steam
Southern Steam
Burlington Steam

Eastern Steam
Lackawanna Steam
Reading Steam
Santa Fe Steam
Union Pacific Steam
Southern Pacific Steam
Milwaukee Steam
Great Northern N. Pacific Steam

Copyright 2000
Robert K. Durham • Auburn, PA 17922

All rights reserved. No part of this book may be reproduced, stored in a retrieval system or transmitted in any form or by any means, electronic, mechanical, photocopying, recording or otherwise, unless authorized in writing by the copyright holder.

Library of Congress Catalog Card Number 99-74785

ISBN 1-891427-05-9

Book #152 of 570

THIS BOOK IS FOR

[signature]
Sept. 26, 2000

Dedication

I dedicate this book to George Eastman, the founder of Eastman Kodak Company. In 1931, he offered a Kodak Brownie Camera to any child who was thirteen years old. I was one of these kids. This camera started me on my way to taking pictures of my neighborhood, and eventually to photograph my favorite thing, trains. Many of my first photos were made with this camera, and are in my first railroad books.

I am indebted to this man, who was a great philanthropist, for giving me the means to start a hobby of collecting railroad photos, and later, putting them into book form. This in order to preserve the fascinating era of steam trains.

PHOTO CREDITS

ROBERT K. DURHAM COLLECTION

J. R. QUINN COLLECTION

REFERENCES

THE HISTORY OF THE WESTERN RAILROADS

JANE ELIOT   CRESCENT BOOKS

CONTENTS
THE ILLINOIS CENTRAL RAILROAD

DESCRIPTION	PAGE
Trains	11 - 19
Switch Engines	20 - 26
Light Passenger	27 - 36
Heavy Passenger	37 - 48
Light Freight	49 - 51
Heavy Freight	52 - 64

ILLINOIS CENTRAL LOCOMOTIVE TYPES IN THIS BOOK
(tabulated by wheel arrangements)

Type	Wheel Arrangement	Name
0-6-0	OOO	6 Wheel Switcher
0-6-0T	OOO	6 Wheel Tank Switcher
0-8-0	OOOO	8 Wheel Switcher
0-8-2	OOOOo	10 Wheel Switcher
2-4-6T	oOOooo	Yard Tank Engine
0-10-0	OOOOO	10 Wheel Switcher
2-6-0	oOOO	Mogul
2-8-0	oOOOO	Consolidation
2-8-2	oOOOOo	Mikado
2-8-4	oOOOOoo	Berkshire
4-4-0	ooOO	American
4-4-2	ooOOo	Atlantic
4-6-0	ooOOO	Ten Wheeler
4-6-2	ooOOOo	Pacific
4-6-4	ooOOOoo	Hudson
4-8-2	ooOOOOo	Mountain
2-10-0	oOOOOO	Decapod
2-10-2	oOOOOOo	Santa Fe
2-6-6-4	oOOO OOOoo	Mallet Articulated

THE ILLINOIS CENTRAL RAILROAD

In 1850, President Millard Fillmore signed a bill giving 2,600, 000 acres of public land to the Illinois Central Railroad. This was on the requirement that Illinois Central would construct 700 miles of track in six years. This act caused much controversy from opponents of the railroad, who thought that the government should not give public lands to private corporations.

The Illinois Central was one of the best known routes to the south from Chicago. It had an impressive array of famous name trains; this fact could have made it difficult for a patron to choose which train to take. It was number one in the field of roads to serve the south from Chicago. The road was proud to serve the finest cuisine in the dining cars; also the best bourbons and liqueurs, rivaling the finest clubs in New Orleans. Many patrons chose the road because of this. The rail.road boasted that, after all, these trains were really hotels on wheels. Therefore, their opulence was well advertised. The fine appointments in the cars consisted of leather arm chairs; a wealth of reading material in the club cars; private valet service; barber shops; telephone service and secretarial service for the business man.

The next page names these trains.

ILLINOIS CENTRAL NAME TRAINS

SOUTH   **NORTH**

South #	Route	Name	North #
#1	CHICAGO-NEW ORLEANS	THE CREOLE	#2
	ST. LOUIS-NEW ORLEANS		#2-202
	LOUISVILLE-NEW ORLEANS		#1-202
#3	CHICAGO-NEW ORLEANS	THE LOUISIANE	#4
#103-3	LOUISVILLE-NEW ORLEANS		#4-104
#5	CHICAGO-NEW ORLEANS	PANAMA	#6
#205-5	ST. LOUIS-NEW ORLEANS	L70	#6-16
		ALL PULLMAN	#6-104 N•ORL-CINC
#7	CHICAGO-MIAMI	FLORIDIAN	#8
#15-7	ST. LOUIS-MIAMI		#8-16
#9	CHICAGO-JAXVL	SEMINOLE	#10
#15-9	ST. LOUIS-JAXVL		#10-16
#15	ST. LOUIS-MEMPHIS	CHICKASAW	#16
#17	CHICAGO-ST. LOUIS	DIAMOND	#18
#19	CHICAGO-ST. LOUIS	DAYLIGHT	#20
#51	CHICAGO-ST. LOUIS	GREEN DIAMOND	#50
#53	CHICAGO-MIAMI	CITY OF MIAMI	#52
#253, 252	ST. LOUIS-CARBONDALE, IL		
#54, 55	CHAMPAGNE, IL-CHICAGO	ILLINI	
#11, 12	CHICAGO-SIOUX CITY	HAWKEYE	
#15, 16	CHICAGO-SIOUX CITY	IOWAN	
#27, 28	CHICAGO-WATERLOO, IA ON YAZOO & MISS. VAL R. R.	SINNISSIPPI	
#15, 12	MEMPHIS-NEW ORLEANS	PLANTER	
#201, 202	MERIDIAN-SHREVEPORT	S.W. LTD	
WEST 203	MERIDIAN-SHREVEPORT	TEXAS LTD	
EAST 204	MERIDIAN-SHREVEPORT	ATLANTA LTD	

ILLINOIS CENTRAL RAILROAD

The first pages will show you some of the trains that ran during this time, starting with a picture of a beautiful ten wheeler, number 2023, hauling her train in the year 1905. Next is number 1004, an Atlantic type, posing for her picture with train around the same period of time. The first car appears to be a combination, baggage and passenger coach. Both of these old timers make a great picture, and their crews must have been very proud of them.

ILLINOIS CENTRAL 2023

ILLINOIS CENTRAL 1004

ILLINOIS CENTRAL 2457
Getting serviced at Jackson, Mississippi, prior to her run. 1943

ILLINOIS CENTRAL 2457 4-8-2
Ready to start her run at Jackson, Mississippi in 1943
Note the mail cars.

ILLINOIS CENTRAL 1074 4-6-2
With her train at Jackson, Mississippi, 1943.
Note the mail car and combination baggage and passenger cars.

ILLINOIS CENTRAL 2305 4-8-2
Highballing her train. This must be a "Hot Shot".
Note the reefers behind the mail car and double tender for long distance.

ILLINOIS CENTRAL 1367 2-8-2
With a mixed freight at Pekin, Illinois in 1941

ILLINOIS CENTRAL 1956 2-8-2
With a mixed freight at Houghton, Louisiana in 1934.

ILLINOIS CENTRAL 2744 2-10-2
With a string of gravel gondolas at Ziegler, Illinois in 1947.

SWITCH ENGINES

ILLINOIS CENTRAL 304 0-6-0
At East St. Louis in 1937.

ILLINOIS CENTRAL 3291 0-6-0 TANK
A beautiful tank engine in the yard at Markham, Illinois in 1950.

ILLINOIS CENTRAL 3551 0-8-0
A large engine for moving heavy trains in the yard.

ILLINOIS CENTRAL 3601 0-10-0
Another heavy engine for moving big loads in the yard.

ILLINOIS CENTRAL 3658 0-8-2
And what sort of monster is this?
It looks like a Mikado that lost its front pilot wheels. Bluford, Illinois, 1955

ILLINOIS CENTRAL 1428 2-4-6 TANK
A very unique engine, and a real beauty.
Looks like she's on the main line with a train.

LIGHT PASSENGER ENGINES

ILLINOIS CENTRAL 572 2-6-0
Jackson, Mississippi 1938

ILLINOIS CENTRAL 3715 2-6-0
Jackson, Mississippi 1938

ILLINOIS CENTRAL 3747 2-6-0
Jackson, Mississippi   1942

ILLINOIS CENTRAL 731 2-6-0
Look at this magnificent example of the builders' art.
It's a shame that such a beauty should be pushing a plow.

ILLINOIS CENTRAL 1464 4-4-0
On the turntable at Onawa, Iowa in 1891.
Note the pole for manually turning the table.

ILLINOIS CENTRAL 4905 4-4-0

ILLINOIS CENTRAL 1022 4-4-2
At the coaling dock, Jackson, Mississippi. 1940

ILLINOIS CENTRAL 1024 4-4-2
At the coaling dock, Jackson, Mississippi. 1940

ILLINOIS CENTRAL 5060 4-6-0
Jackson, Mississippi 1937

HEAVY PASSENGER ENGINES

ILLINOIS CENTRAL 997 4-6-2
Jackson, Mississippi 1938

ILLINOIS CENTRAL 1104 4-6-2
Jackson, Mississippi 1938

ILLINOIS CENTRAL 1110 4-6-2

ILLINOIS CENTRAL 1146 4-6-2
An attempt to streamline by the I. C. shops.

ILLINOIS CENTRAL 1191 4-6-2
Jackson, Mississippi 1938

ILLINOIS CENTRAL 1203 4-6-2
St. Louis, Missouri 1936

ILLINOIS CENTRAL 2065 4-6-2
Paducah, Kentucky 1956

ILLINOIS CENTRAL #1 4-6-4

Centralia, IL 1939

ILLINOIS CENTRAL 2350 4-8-2
Bluford, Illinois 1949

ILLINOIS CENTRAL 2409 4-8-2

ILLINOIS CENTRAL 2446 4-8-2
Paducah, Kentucky 1949

LIGHT FREIGHT ENGINES

ILLINOIS CENTRAL 769 2-8-0
East St. Louis, Illinois 1939

ILLINOIS CENTRAL 907 2-8-0
Kankakee, Illinois 1956

HEAVY FREIGHT ENGINES

ILLINOIS CENTRAL 1447 2-8-2
Freeport, Illinois 1952

ILLINOIS CENTRAL 1450 2-8-2

ILLINOIS CENTRAL 1977 2-8-2
East St. Louis, Illinois 1936

ILLINOIS CENTRAL 2127 2-8-2
Paducah, Kentucky 1937

ILLINOIS CENTRAL 7014 2-8-4
Bluford, Illinois 1939

ILLINOIS CENTRAL 7028 2-8-4
Asylum, Mississippi 1938

ILLINOIS CENTRAL 8038 2-8-4
Bluford, Illinois 1938

ILLINOIS CENTRAL 8045 2-8-4
Bluford, Illinois 1949

ILLINOIS CENTRAL 3611 2-10-0
Bluford, Illinois 1956

ILLINOIS CENTRAL 2804 2-10-2
Chicago, Illinois 1932

ILLINOIS CENTRAL 3103 2-10-2
Chicago, Illinois 1932

ILLINOIS CENTRAL 6068 2-6-6-4
1934